El Amigo Eterno

Written by Isabella Lindia
Illustrated by Ava Lindia

Creo En Ti

Había una vez, una niña que se llamaba Bernadette vivía en un pueblo pequeño en la selva Amazónica.

Once upon a time, there was a young girl named Bernadette who lived in a small village in the Amazon jungle.

Bernadette se sentía muy sola. No tenía hermanos y sus padres trabajaban mucho.

Bernadette often felt very lonely. She had no siblings and her parents worked a lot.

Siempre quería una mascota para hacerle compañía - un gato, un perro o incluso un pez. Pero sus padres no lo permitían.

She always wanted a pet to keep her company- a cat, a dog, or even a fish. But her parents did not allow this.

Una mañana, Bernadette se despertó y fue a la ventana para abrir sus cortinas. El sol brillaba tanto.

One morning, Bernadette woke up and went to the window to open her curtains. The sun was shining so bright.

Escuchó un ruido suave y miró hacia abajo a los rieles de la ventana. Un pájaro pequeño estaba sentado ahí intentando a mover sus alas pero estaba herido y no pudo volar. Bernadette decidió dejarlo y chequearlo durante el día pensando que el pájaro se iba a mejorar.

She heard a faint noise and looked down at the windowsill. A small bird sat on the ledge, trying to flap its wings but it was injured and could not fly. Bernadette decided to leave the bird alone and check up on it throughout the day thinking that maybe it would get better and fly away.

Más tarde esa noche, Bernadette chequeó por los rieles de la ventana y el pájaro seguía ahí, haciendo sonidos débiles.

Later that night, Bernadette checked the windowsill and the bird was still there, quietly chirping.

Tuvo una idea: Bernadette fue a su cómoda y buscó una media en su cajón. Ella encontró una media morada que era del tamaño perfecto.

She had an idea: Bernadette dug into the bottom of her sock drawer to find an old, single, purple sock. It was the perfect size.

Abrió la ventana y extendió su brazo cuidadosamente para recoger al pájaro. El pájaro caminó sobre la mano de Bernadette y ella lo agarró suavemente.

She opened her window, and reached her arm out to gently pick up the bird. It crawled right into her palm, and her fingers lightly grasped it.

Bernadette puso el pájaro en la media morada para que se mantuviera caliente.

Bernadette put the bird into the purple sock to keep it warm.

Luego, ella puso la media en una caja pequeña, donde el pájaro se quedó por la siguiente semana. Ella puso un plato de agua en la caja, junto con algunas migajas de pan.

Then, she placed the sock in a small box, where it stayed for the next week. She put a dish of water in the box, along with some breadcrumbs.

Todas las noches, Bernadette cuidaba al pájaro. Lo cuidaba por varios días y por el proceso, se convirtieron en mejores amigos.

Every night, Bernadette checked on the bird and took care of it. She did this for several days and throughout the process, they became best friends.

Un día, ella escuchó un sonido proveniente de la caja, y ella entendió que el pájaro ya estaba listo para volar.

One day, she heard a loud and high chirp come from the box. She understood that the bird was ready to fly.

Bernadette no quería liberarlo, pero ella decidió que era mejor para el pájaro.

Bernadette didn't want to let it go, but she decided it was best for the bird.

Ella sostuvo el pájaro entre sus manos y abrió la ventana. De manera inmediata, el pájaro movió sus alas y se fue. ¡Podía volar de nuevo!

Holding the bird in her hands, she opened the window. Immediately, the bird flapped its wings and took off. It could fly again!

Bernadette sonrió, pero realmente estaba triste. Pensaba que nunca iba a volver a ver al pájaro de nuevo. Por fin ella se estaba sintiendo que ya no estaba sola por la compañía del pájaro, pero ahora se había ido.

Bernadette smiled, but she was truly sad. She thought she would never see the bird again. She finally felt like she wasn't alone anymore, but now the bird had gone.

Sin embargo, desde ese día, el pájaro visitaba a Bernadette en la ventana de su dormitorio, cantándole buenos días.

However, from that day on, the bird visited Bernadette on her bedroom windowsill, chirping good morning.

El Fin

The End

This story is dedicated to the memory of Bernadette Louise DeLong (January 1, 1950 - April 26, 2020), our first art teacher, who taught us that with creativity, everything old becomes new again.

Creo En Ti Media

www.creoentimedia.com

Text Copyright © 2022 Isabella Lindia

Images Copyright © 2022 Ava Lindia

ISBN-13: (paperback) 978-1-949929-80-5

Library of Congress Control Number- In production

Creo En Ti

All rights reserved. No part of this publication may be reproduced, distributed, or transmitted in any form or by any means, including photocopying, recording, or other electronic or mechanical methods, without the prior written permission of the publisher, except in the case of brief quotations embodied in critical reviews and certain other noncommercial uses permitted by copyright law.

Author & Illustrator

Isabella and Ava Lindia attend Ursuline Academy in Wilmington, Delaware and will be graduating in June of 2022. They are twin sisters who share a love for creative writing and design. Their inspiration for this book can be attributed to their very first art teacher, as well as their involvement with the Global Scholars Program at their high school. Their future plans include attending college and using their creativity in everyday life. They hope their readers will take away from their story that everyone has the ability to make the world a better place.

Isabella Lindia, Author

Ava Lindia, Illustrator

About Creo En Ti Media

Creo En Ti is a Spanish phrase which means "I believe in you." Creo En Ti Media began in Lisa Pietropola's AP Spanish class at Northern High School in South Central Pennsylvania as a student-centered, bilingual literacy project designed to promote early childhood literacy. It developed into a cross-curricular endeavor combining art and foreign language content areas. This project created an opportunity for outstanding student work to be published and available to children and educators. Creo En Ti Media strives to give parents and educators the tools to spark an interest in language learning at a young age.

For more information about this project, including lesson plans for Spanish language classes, ESL classes and activities for parents and early childhood educators, please visit our website at www.creoentimedia.com

"Creo en ti means so much more than simply 'I believe in you.' It is the pillar of my teaching philosophy. Educators, like parents, pour their hearts and souls into the growth and success of their children. Students need to be filled with a sense of security before learning can take place. That is where Creo en ti comes in."
–Lisa Pietropola

Creo En Ti
www.creoentimedia.com

Our Creative Director

Lisa Pietropola is the Creative Director of Creo En Ti Media and has spent 15 years in both the public and private school systems advocating for world languages. Lisa has built her career on establishing confidence in her students and using that confidence to empower lives. The recipient of the Outstanding Teacher of the Year Award, 2017, Lisa holds a Master of Arts degree in Spanish from Saint Louis University, Madrid, Spain. Lisa's years living abroad molded her approach to language learning. She continues to teach and inspire students today and is certified in both Spanish and English as a Second Language. Along with leading educational trips abroad, Lisa enjoys traveling with her husband and their two daughters.

"I am most proud of this endeavor not only because of the empowerment of second language learning, but also because we are raising a generation of students who have educators who believe in them."
–Lisa Pietropola

Made in United States
Orlando, FL
12 March 2022

15699771R00022